THE FAIRY TALE COOKBOOK

by Carol MacGregor

illustrated by Debby L. Carter

Macmillan Publishing Co., Inc.
New York

Collier Macmillan Publishers
London

10 9 8 7 6 5 4 3 2 1

LIBRARY OF CONGRESS CATALOGING IN PUBLICATION DATA

MacGregor, Carol.   The fairy tale cookbook.

SUMMARY: A collection of recipes for a variety of dishes based
on such well-known tales as "The three bears," "Hansel and
Gretel," and "Stone soup." Each recipe is introduced by a
brief summary of the original tale.
1. Cookery—Juvenile literature. [1. Cookery]
I. Carter, Debby L., ill. II. Title.
TX652.5.M247 641.5′123 82-7742 ISBN 0-02-761970-2 AACR2

TEXT ACKNOWLEDGMENTS
The author is grateful for permission to reproduce text excerpts
from the following copyrighted materials:
"The Three Bears" from *The Three Bears* by Paul Galdone. Copyright © 1972
by the author, and used by permission of Houghton Mifflin/Clarion Books, New
York; "The Pancake" from *The Pancake* by Anita Lobel. Copyright © 1978 by
Anita Lobel. By permission of Greenwillow Books (A Division of William
Morrow & Co., Inc.); "Snow White and the Seven Dwarfs" from *Snow White and
the Seven Dwarfs, a Tale from the Brothers Grimm,* translated by Randall
Jarrell, pictures by Nancy Ekholm Burkert. Published by Farrar, Straus &
Giroux, Inc., 1972. Reprinted by permission of Farrar, Straus & Giroux, Inc.;
"The Princess and the Pea" from *Seven Tales* by Hans Christian Andersen,
translated by Eva LeGallienne. Courtesy of Harper & Row, Publishers, Inc.; "The
Three Billy Goats Gruff" from *The Three Billy Goats Gruff,* © 1957 by Marcia
Brown. Reprinted by permission of Harcourt Brace Jovanovich, Inc.; "Puss in
Boots" from *Puss in Boots,* retold and illustrated by Marcia Brown. Copyright
1952 by Marcia Brown; copyright renewed. (New York: Charles Scribner's Sons,
1952) Reprinted with the permission of Charles Scribner's Sons; "Strega Nona"
from *Strega Nona* by Tomie de Paola. © 1975 by Tomie de Paola. Published by
(Continued on page 86)

For Dr. Winkelstein,
who truly cared about my happiness

ACKNOWLEDGMENTS

With fondness and appreciation for Gwyneth Olsen, who tested the recipes and made unique suggestions, and to Ms. Dolores Vogliano, children s librarian at the Yorkville Branch of the New York Public Library, for all her kind assistance with the research involved with the book.

—C. M.

⋖§ CONTENTS §⋗

VEGETABLES AND FRUITS

DINNERS

SWEETS AND THINGS

BREADS

❧ INTRODUCTION ❧

Cooking is a wonderful means of creative expression as well as a practical skill. It is especially rewarding because you can share your creations with your family or friends. Preparing recipes concerned with your favorite fairy-tale characters allows you to make your thoughts and feelings about them real. How would you like the French soldiers' stone soup to taste or Cinderella's wedding cake to look?

A recipe should give you all the basic ingredients and instructions for the dish you are making, but it is your special touch with seasonings or frosting decorations that makes each dish your own special version.

One word of advice: Read the recipe all the way through before cooking, so you can picture what you are going to do. Get out all the ingredients called for, placing them in the area where you are going to work, in the order in which you are going to use them. Clean up at various stages as you go along since you may need to use the measuring cups or bowls more than once.

Enjoy reading the fairy tales, perhaps again, and the fun of sharing the tales and recipes with your guests. The excerpts from some of my favorite versions are found in italics in each recipe.

⊰ BREAKFASTS ⊱

The Little Wee Bear's Special Porridge

from "The Three Bears"

A family of three bears lived happily in the woods—Little Wee Baby Bear, Medium-sized Mama Bear and Great Big Papa Bear. They each had their very own porridge bowl, spoon, chair, and bed that was just the right size for each. One morning, while their steaming porridge was cooling, they took a stroll in the woods. While they were out, Goldilocks, a golden-haired little girl, discovered their home and decided to explore. When she came upon the porridge, it smelled so delicious she had to taste it. The big bowl was much too hot. The middle-sized bowl was much too cold.

Then she tasted the porridge of the Little Wee Bear. It was just right. Goldilocks liked it so much that she ate it all up.

Then Goldilocks tried all the chairs and all the beds for size. Each time, the Little Wee Bear's suited her perfectly. Soon she fell asleep in his bed—only to be awakened by the family when they returned. Startled, she fled and the three bears never saw her again.

What made the Little Wee Bear's porridge so special were the bananas, nuts, and shredded coconut he always added.

INGREDIENTS

1⅓ cups rolled oats (regular or instant)
½ teaspoon salt
3 cups milk
1 banana
½ cup chopped walnuts
¼ cup shredded coconut or
  3 tablespoons brown
  sugar (optional)
milk

UTENSILS

medium-sized saucepan with cover
measuring spoons
measuring cups
large serving spoon
dull knife

1. Cook rolled oats with $\frac{1}{2}$ teaspoon salt according to package directions, using milk.
2. Peel banana, cut it into thin slices with a dull knife, and place slices on top of porridge.
3. Add walnuts. Stir nuts and banana slices into porridge. Spoon porridge into serving dishes.
4. Sprinkle coconut or brown sugar on top of porridge. Serve hot with milk. Makes 4 servings.

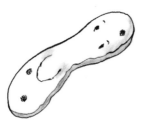

Blueberry Pancakes

from "The Pancake"

Seven hungry children stood eagerly around the stove waiting to eat the wonderful pancake their mother was cooking for them. She insisted that they be patient.

"Before we eat, I must flip the pancake over and cook it on the other side."

When the pancake heard that it was to be eaten, it jumped out of the pan and rolled like a wheel through the door and onto the road.

The runaway pancake rolled and rolled and rolled, escaping the foolish farmer, the silly goose, the dim-witted cat, and others —but not the pig!

You can have fun flipping over your own pancakes—but be careful none jump out of the pan and escape!

INGREDIENTS	UTENSILS
3 tablespoons butter or margarine	saucepan
	measuring spoons
¾ cup milk	large bowl
1 egg	beater
1 cup all-purpose flour	measuring cups
2 teaspoons baking powder	medium bowl
2 tablespoons sugar	large spoon
½ teaspoon salt	large frying pan
½ cup fresh or canned blueberries	spatula
	large plate
butter, syrup, or powdered sugar	

1. Turn on oven and set at 200° F.
2. In a small saucepan, melt butter or margarine—slowly, so that it will not burn. Set aside.

3. In a large bowl, lightly beat together milk, egg, and 2 table-spoons melted butter or margarine.

4. In a medium bowl, mix together with the large spoon flour, baking powder, sugar, and salt. Add this mixture to the first mixture and stir in well.

5. Fold in blueberries. (If using canned blueberries, drain well before using.)

6. Place a small amount of remaining butter or margarine in the frying pan. Heat until very hot—the pan is hot enough when drops of water bounce after hitting the pan's surface. Drop about 2 tablespoons of batter onto the center of the frying pan and smooth it out into a 4-inch pancake. Cook until bubbles form on the top and underside is lightly browned. Turn over with a spatula and brown on the other side. Add additional butter if necessary.

7. Stack the pancakes on the plate and keep them warm in oven until ready to serve. Serve with butter, syrup, or powdered sugar. Makes 12 medium-sized pancakes.

The Wicked Queen's Poison Baked Apples

from "Snow White and the Seven Dwarfs"

The seven dwarfs who lived in the forest and mined in the mountains treasure Snow White, a beautiful young princess who has escaped from her jealous and evil stepmother, who tried to have her killed. The dwarfs rightly fear that the wicked queen will learn that Snow White still lives and will try to kill her again. Unfortunately, their fears come true. The queen's magic mirror tells her the truth—Snow White is alive and more beautiful than she. Enraged, the queen, disguised as an old peddler-woman, twice tries to kill her young rival—to no avail.

Then she went to a very secret, lonely room that no one ever came to, and there she made a poisoned apple. On the outside it was beautiful, so that anyone who saw it wanted it; but whoever ate even the least bite of it would die.

The wicked queen finally tricks Snow White into taking a bite of the apple, and she appears to die. In great sadness, the dwarfs lay her in a glass coffin on the hill, where she remains perfectly still but radiantly beautiful. One day, a handsome prince finds her and persuades the dwarfs to give him Snow White. When the coffin is moved, the piece of apple is dislodged from her throat, causing her to come back to life. She marries the prince, and the mean queen is dispensed with.

The baked apples you can make from this recipe will look just like the poison one made for Snow White—but yours will taste delicious and won't harm anyone.

INGREDIENTS

4 firm apples (Delicious or Cortland)
1 8-ounce bottle grenadine syrup (sweet cherry flavoring)
heavy cream

UTENSILS

paring knife
apple corer
small bowl
medium baking dish
large spoon
cooling rack

1. Turn on oven and set at 375° F.
2. Peel skin off the top third of each apple.
3. Remove core from each apple with the apple corer. Be careful not to pierce the bottom, so the center can be filled.
4. Pour half the grenadine into a small bowl (save the rest for preparing this recipe another time). Separately place each apple with peeled side down into the grenadine for 10 minutes to soak up the red color and flavor.
5. Place apples, peeled side up, close together in baking dish. Fill centers with the grenadine the apples have been soaking in.
6. Fill baking dish with ½ inch water. Put apples in the oven and bake for 20 minutes or until soft when pricked with a fork.
7. Remove apples from oven and set baking dish on the cooling rack. Serve warm or cold with plain or whipped cream. Makes 4 servings.

❦ LUNCHES ❧

The Goats Gruff
Meadow Salad

from "The Three Billy Goats Gruff"

Once there was a family of three billy goats named Gruff. They yearned to go up on the hillside to enjoy the sweet grasses and the wild vegetables that grew there. However, to reach this lush meadow, they had to cross a bridge under which lived a huge, mean troll who let it be known that he was most eager to dine on them. Finally, they managed to trick the troll and go up into the fragrant meadow.

There the billy goats got so fat they were scarcely able to walk again; and if the fat hasn't fallen off them, why, they're still fat. . . .

The goats' salad was perfectly prepared for them by Mother Nature, but you will have to gather the fresh ingredients for your meadow salad. The feta cheese is made from goat's milk and is mild and tasty. When eating it, remember the Billy Goats Gruffs' cleverness in tricking the troll.

INGREDIENTS

1 small head Boston lettuce
1 small bunch watercress
8 cherry tomatoes
6 medium radishes
2 medium carrots
1/4 pound feta (goat) cheese
    (if unavailable, use
    Cheddar cheese)

UTENSILS

paring knife
paper towels
medium-sized salad bowl
grater

1. Cut the bottom off the head of lettuce. Wash leaves carefully under cold water, throwing away any damaged ones. Pat dry with paper towels. Arrange leaves attractively in a

circular fashion around salad bowl, putting the larger leaves on the outside and the smaller leaves on the bottom.

2. Snap off 10 small stems with leaves from the larger stems of the watercress. Throw away the large stems. Wash the leafy stems under cold water. Pat dry with paper towels. Set aside.
3. Wash all the vegetables under cold water.
4. Remove stems from cherry tomatoes. Cut in half. Arrange among the smaller lettuce leaves.
5. Cut tops and bottoms off the radishes and slice them thin. Place radishes among lettuce and tomatoes.
6. Cut tops and bottoms off carrots. Grate. Sprinkle over the salad.
7. Crumble feta cheese over salad. Top with watercress. Toss with dressing. Makes 4 servings.

French Dressing

INGREDIENTS   UTENSILS

6 tablespoons vegetable oil   small jar with lid cover
2 tablespoons vinegar   measuring spoons
¼ teaspoon mustard
¼ teaspoon salt
dash of pepper

1. Put all salad dressing ingredients in a jar. Cover tightly, shake well, and refrigerate. When ready to serve, shake again and pour over the salad.
2. Toss salad lightly, cutting the larger outside leaves into smaller pieces and mixing them in.

12

The Queen's
Cream of Pea Soup

from "The Princess and the Pea"

The prince very much wanted to be married—but only to a real princess. He made many long journeys, all which were unsuccessful because he could not tell whether any of the princesses he met were genuine. One night, a horrendous storm brought a rain-soaked and destitute maiden to the town gates where the prince lived. The king, hearing of the girl's plight, went to see what the disturbance was and brought the girl to his castle. Despite her appearance, the girl kept insisting that she was a true princess.

"We'll soon find out about that," said the old queen. She didn't say a word to anyone, but went straight to the guest room; there she took all the bedclothes off the bed and carefully placed a tiny pea under the mattress. She piled twenty mattresses on top of it, and on top of the twenty mattresses she piled twenty down comforters, and then she went back and told the princess that her bed was ready.

The maiden couldn't sleep at all and tossed and turned throughout the night. In the morning she complained of her bruises. Then the queen and the prince knew that she was indeed a princess—no one else could be so tender.

This royal recipe for rich pea soup will warm you and your friends on any stormy evening—and you won't have any problems sleeping through the night.

INGREDIENTS	UTENSILS
2 tablespoons chopped onion	paring knife
2 tablespoons butter or margarine	measuring spoons
	saucepan
2 9-ounce packages frozen peas	large spoon
	electric blender or strainer
½ teaspoon sugar	measuring cups
⅓ cup water	
1 cup light cream	
⅛ teaspoon salt	

1. Peel and chop an onion. Measure out 2 tablespoons.
2. In a saucepan, melt butter or margarine slowly so that it does not burn. Add chopped onion and cook until golden in color, stirring constantly to keep it from burning.
3. Add peas, sugar, and water. Cook about 10 minutes until peas are tender.
4. Put pea mixture in an electric blender and blend, or push mixture through a strainer. Return to saucepan.
5. Add cream and salt. Reheat before serving. Makes 6 cups.

The Marquis of Carabas's Rabbit

from "Puss in Boots"

A poor miller died and left his three sons what few belongings he had. The youngest received not the mill, not the ass, but Puss, the family cat blessed with a wild imagination. Immediately, Puss decided to prove to the son that he was the best of all the miller's possessions. He requested a pair of boots and set out to impress the king. On his way, he snared a wild rabbit and proceeded to present it with great flair to His Highness, pretending his penniless owner had a plentiful warren.

Bowing low before His Majesty, he said, "Here, Sire, is a wild rabbit from the warren of my lord, the Marquis of Carabas." (That was the name Puss was pleased to give his master.)

16

Puss continued to impress the king with his master's false wealth, implying that the marquis owned acres of land for hunting, wheat fields full of great amounts of grain, and even a magnificent castle. The king was so delighted that he finally offered his daughter's hand in marriage to the marquis.

You, too, can do some pretending when you invite friends to a lunch of "rabbit." What you will actually be serving will be a delicious dish of melted cheese traditionally served on toast which Welsh families eat when they have not been lucky enough to catch the real thing. They call the dish "Welsh Rabbit."

INGREDIENTS	UTENSILS
½ pound processed Cheddar cheese	paring knife
	double boiler
¾ cup light cream	measuring cups
1 teaspoon Worcestershire sauce	measuring spoons
	large spoon
½ teaspoon dry mustard	toaster
4 slices bread	

1. Cut cheese into thin slices and place them in the top of a double boiler.
2. Add cream, Worcestershire sauce, and mustard. Cook over medium heat, stirring occasionally, until cheese has melted.
3. Toast 4 slices of bread and place each slice on a separate plate.
4. Pour some of the hot melted cheese mixture over each piece of toast. Makes 4 servings.

Strega Nona's Magic Pasta

from "Strega Nona"

Strega Nona (which means "Grandma Witch" in Italian) pos-
sessed such unique magical powers that all the townsfolk sought
out her cures. Among other things, she could make her pot
produce pasta upon her command. As Strega Nona was getting
older, she hired a local village boy, Big Arthur, to help with
the household and gardening chores, and sternly warned him
never to touch her pasta pot. One day when Strega Nona was
away visiting a friend, Big Arthur could not resist the tempta-
tion to be the town's hero and present the citizens with all the
pasta they could eat. He dared to say Strega Nona's magic words
to the pot:

Bubble, bubble, pasta pot.
Boil me up some pasta, nice and hot.
I'm hungry and it's time to sup.
Boil enough pasta to fill me up.

The pot did indeed bubble, bubble, and boil, until soon the town was almost buried in an avalanche of pasta. Happily, Strega Nona arrived just in time to save the day!

This pasta recipe is easy to make and is guaranteed not to increase on its own—unless you, like Strega Nona, happen to possess magical powers.

INGREDIENTS

2 tablespoons finely chopped
   yellow onion
¼ pound boiled ham
4 tablespoons butter or
   margarine
1 teaspoon salt
dash of pepper
½ 9-ounce package frozen peas
1 cup heavy cream
4 ounces white fettucini
   noodles
4 ounces green fettucini
   noodles
⅓ cup grated Parmesan
   cheese

UTENSILS

paring knife
measuring spoons
large frying pan
large spoon
measuring cups
large (5-quart) pot
colander or large strainer

1. Peel and chop an onion. Measure out 2 tablespoons.
2. Remove skin, if there is any, from outside of ham. Cut ham into small pieces.
3. In a frying pan, melt 2 tablespoons of butter or margarine slowly over medium heat and watch that it does not burn. Cook chopped onion and chopped ham in the butter until onion is golden yellow.
4. Add salt and pepper and mix in well.
5. Add peas. Continue to cook for another 5 minutes.
6. Add ½ cup of heavy cream and cook approximately 5 minutes or until cream thickens slightly. Set aside.
7. Fill the large pot with 3 quarts of hot water. Bring to a boil. Add white and green noodles. Bring water to a boil again and cook, uncovered, for 7 minutes. Be sure to watch noodles as they are cooking because they can easily boil over.
8. Drain noodles in a colander or strainer. Run cold water over them quickly to stop the cooking.
9. Add noodles to ham-and-pea mixture. Then add remaining 2 tablespoons butter and remaining ½ cup cream. Turn heat on low and toss noodles with other ingredients until noodles are well covered with butter and cream.
10. Add Parmesan cheese to the mixture and stir in well.
11. When all ingredients are completely heated through, serve hot. Makes 4 servings.

The French Soldiers' Beef Stew

from "Stone Soup"

Three very hungry and very tired French soldiers wandered into a town. The poor peasants, seeing them coming and fearing the worst, hid all of their food. When the soldiers asked for something to eat, the townsfolk all said that because of a poor harvest, their cupboards were empty. The soldiers, guessing that they were lying, casually announced that they would make "stone soup." The peasants, being curious, gathered around. The soldiers asked for a huge cooking pot full of water, firewood, and some stones, all of which were brought to them. Then they asked for salt and pepper, and some carrots. Then they said:

"If we had a bit of beef and a few potatoes, this soup would be good enough for a rich man's table."

The ingredients were hastily contributed, along with a goodly amount of bread and cider. Then a huge banquet took place with much eating and dancing and singing, all because of this marvelous soup made from stones.

You, too, can make a marvelous beef stew that provides good reason for celebration. The only ingredient *not* needed is the stones.

INGREDIENTS

3 tablespoons butter or
   margarine
2 pounds chuck beef, cut into
   1½-inch cubes
10 small carrots
10 small white onions
8 small potatoes
1 10-ounce package frozen
   peas

UTENSILS

large frying pan
measuring spoons
large slotted spoon
paring knife
vegetable peeler
2-quart casserole with cover
measuring cups
large spoon

22

1 tablespoon flour
2 tablespoons tomato sauce
1 tablespoon vinegar
1½ teaspoons salt
⅛ teaspoon pepper
⅛ teaspoon thyme
dash of garlic powder
1 bay leaf
1 10½-ounce can beef
    consommé
1 cup water

1. Turn on oven and set at 350° F.
2. In a large frying pan, melt the butter or margarine. Add the beef and keep the pieces separated with your spoon. Brown well on all sides. Turn over with the slotted spoon so as not to pierce the meat and release the juices. Set aside.
3. Cut the tops and bottoms off the carrots. Scrape the skin off with the vegetable peeler. Set aside.
4. Peel the onions and potatoes. Set aside.
5. Layer the beef, carrots, onions, and potatoes in the casserole.
6. Add the peas.
7. Stir the flour into the butter and scrapings in the bottom of the frying pan and cook for 1 minute over low heat. Add the tomato sauce, vinegar, salt, pepper, thyme, garlic powder, and bay leaf. Add the consommé and water.
8. Bring the mixture to a boil and pour over the beef and vegetables. Cover and bake in the oven for 1½ hours or until the meat is very tender. Makes 4 generous servings.

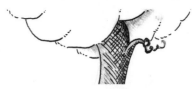

❧ VEGETABLES AND FRUITS ❧

Jack's Favorite String Beans with Apple Cubes

from "Jack and the Beanstalk"

Young Jack lived with his widowed mother in a small cottage. He dearly loved her but was lazy and chose not to work. Soon their savings were gone and the mother had to sell their last possession, the cow. Jack was given the responsibility to take the cow to town and to make the best sale he could. But along the way he became fascinated with an offer of magic beans, and he traded the cow for them. His mother was furious. Throwing

the beans out the window, she sent him to bed without supper. In the morning, Jack looked outside.

The magic beans had grown into a great beanstalk, which went up and up, twining and twisting, till it reached the sky. . . .

Jack climbed the beanstalk and at the top he found a giant ogre. He managed to trick him out of golden coins, a golden goose that laid golden eggs, and a golden harp. This so enraged the ogre that he tried to follow Jack down the beanstalk, but clever Jack cut the stalk and the giant was killed.

Owing to his good fortune, string beans became Jack's favorite food. This is a different and tasty recipe for them that might become one of your favorites.

INGREDIENTS

1 tart apple (McIntosh or
    Granny Smith)
2 tablespoons butter or
    margarine
1/2 cup light cream
1 1/8 teaspoons salt
dash of pepper
1 pound fresh green string
    beans or 1 9-ounce pack-
    age frozen green beans
1 cup water

UTENSILS

paring knife
apple corer
measuring spoons
2 saucepans, 1 with cover
measuring cups
colander or strainer

1. Peel and core apples. Cut into small cubes.
2. Melt butter or margarine in one of the saucepans. Be careful not to let it burn. Add apple cubes and cover over medium heat for 5 minutes or until they are tender.
3. Add cream, ⅛ teaspoon salt, and pepper. Set aside.
4. If using fresh beans, rinse and drain them in the colander. Snap ends off and cut beans into 3-inch pieces.
5. In the other saucepan, put the water and 1 teaspoon salt. Bring to a boil. Place fresh or frozen beans in the water. Lower heat so that water simmers and cover pan. Cook fresh beans for 10 to 12 minutes or until tender; cook frozen beans for about 5 minutes. Drain beans in colander or strainer.
6. Add cooked beans to apple mixture. Stir together. Reheat and serve hot. Makes 4 to 6 servings.

Aladdin's Jeweled
Fruit Ambrosia

from "Aladdin and the Wonderful Lamp"

A dishonest African magician reads of a magic lamp hidden in Persia. However, to work its magic it has to be stolen by someone else. The magician chooses Aladdin, a good but lazy Persian boy, who lives with his widowed mother, to find and steal the lamp. The magician then tells Aladdin how to lift the stone from the secret cave, lower himself down, and proceed through three halls, the last being filled with beautiful fruit trees, to find the lamp. To aid him, the magician gives Aladdin a magic ring for protection. Aladdin finds the lamp, and as he leaves he picks some fruit from the trees. When Aladdin arrives at the entrance of the cave, he refuses to give up the lamp until the magician lifts him out. The magician, enraged, slams the stone shut and leaves the boy to die. Accidentally, Aladdin rubs the ring and the Genie of the Ring appears and grants Aladdin's wish to be home. Once he is home, his mother absentmindedly rubs the lamp and releases the Genie of the Lamp—the most powerful of all the genies. He grants them their wish for money, which they desperately need.

After a while, Aladdin falls in love with the sultan's daughter. He tells his mother to go and ask for her hand in marriage on his behalf.

The poor woman said that he must be crazy; but her son not only knew what a treasure he had in the magic lamp, but also how valuable were the shining fruits he gathered, which he thought at the time to be colored glass. At first he sent a bowlful of these jewels—for so they were—to the sultan. . . .

Before he gives up his daughter, the sultan makes many demands, all of which are met by the Genie of the Lamp. In time, Aladdin and the princess are married.

You can use the fruit that became jewels to make a beautiful first course or dessert. The honeydew melon balls are emeralds, the strawberries are rubies, and the deep blue grapes are sapphires. The coconut and the cinnamon garnishes are typical Near Eastern touches. (If you cannot find a honeydew melon or the blue grapes, use green seedless grapes for emeralds and blueberries for sapphires).

INGREDIENTS	UTENSILS
1 small honeydew melon	large knife
20 medium-sized dark blue grapes	large spoon
	melon baller or teaspoon
1/2 pint strawberries	large glass bowl
1/4 cup shredded coconut	strainer
ground cinnamon	paring knife
1/2 cup orange juice (optional)	measuring cups

1. Cut honeydew melon crosswise with large knife into two round halves. Remove the seeds with large spoon and discard.
2. With the large scoop of melon baller or a teaspoon, scoop out melon balls as close to each other as possible to get as many as possible. You will get about 25 balls from each half. Place in large bowl.
3. Wash grapes and strawberries in strainer under cold water.
4. Cut the grapes in half with paring knife and remove the seeds with the point of knife. Place in large bowl.
5. Remove the stems from the strawberries with paring knife. Slice the large strawberries but leave the medium ones whole. Place in bowl.

6. Pour orange juice over the fruit if desired and then toss the fruit. Sprinkle top with coconut and several dashes of cinnamon.
7. Place in refrigerator to chill until ready to serve. You may serve from the bowl at the table or fill individual glass bowls ahead of time. Makes 8 servings.

Ananse's Baked Yams and Peaches for the African Fairy

from "A Story, a Story"

Once, a long time ago in Africa, Ananse, the Spider Man, wanted to buy the wonderful stories of Nyame, the Sky God. Ananse spun a spider's web to the sky and paid the god a visit. There he learned that to obtain the stories, he had to complete three impossible tasks: to bring to the Sky God Osebo, the

Leopard of the Terrible Teeth; Mmboro, the Hornet Who Stings Like Fire; and Mmoatia, the Fairy Whom Men Never See. Ananse cleverly caught the Leopard and the Hornet and then set about to capture the Mmoatia, the Fairy. He carved a wooden doll, covered it with gum, and placed a bowl of yams in its hands. Mmoatia came upon the doll and said:

> *"Gum baby, I am hungry. May I eat some of your yams?"*
> *Ananse pulled the vine in his hiding place so that the doll seemed to nod its head. So the Fairy took the bowl from the doll. . . .*

While eating the yams, the Fairy became stuck to the doll because of the gum covering it. Ananse captured her and with the others returned to the Sky God. The Sky God honored his word and gave the stories to the Spider Man which children enjoy to this day.

Sliced yams layered with peaches make an excellent casserole side dish, particularly with chicken or turkey. And you needn't be a Fairy whom men never see to enjoy them.

INGREDIENTS

3 medium yams (about 1/2
    pound) or 2 17-ounce
    canned yams
3 medium ripe peaches or
    1 20-ounce can Freestone
    peach halves

UTENSILS

large pot
large fork
medium bowl
paring knife
9-inch pie plate or casserole
    dish

¼ stick butter or margarine measuring cups
¼ cup sugar measuring spoons
½ teaspoon vanilla
⅛ teaspoon cinnamon

1. Turn on oven and set at 350° F.
2. Fill the pot half full of warm water and place on the stove.
3. Wash yams and put them in the pot. Bring water to a boil and then turn down heat to medium. Cook yams in simmering water for about 1 hour or until tender but not soft.
4. Remove yams from water with a large fork. Place in the bowl and allow to cool.
5. Peel peaches. Cut in halves, cutting from top to bottom. Remove stones. If using canned peaches, drain off juice.
6. Butter the pie plate or casserole with 1 tablespoon butter or margarine. Peel skin off yams. Cut yams into ¼-inch slices, and layer bottom of pie plate or casserole dish with half of the yam slices. If using canned yams, drain off water and proceed as with fresh yams.
7. Place peach halves over the layer of yams.
8. Place remaining yam slices over peaches.
9. Cut butter or margarine into small pieces and arrange over top of layer of yams.
10. Sprinkle sugar over the whole top of the casserole.
11. Sprinkle vanilla and cinnamon over the top of the sugar.
12. Bake in oven for 1 hour or until the sugar becomes brown and sticky. Makes 6 to 8 servings.

❧ DINNERS ❧

The Wealthy Man's
Sweet and Sour Pork

from "The Shady Tree"

There was never a question that the wealthy man owned the huge cypress tree that grew outside of his grand house.

After dinner the wealthy man would go out and sit under the shade of the tree to enjoy an occasional breeze.

The question put to a court of law was whether he owned the shade from the tree. The rich man thought that he did and, in his greed, sold it to a poor peddler who briefly sat in its shade. The peddler then asserted his right to sit in his shade wherever it went—even if this meant the wealthy man's bedroom! The court agreed with the peddler.

This intriguing tale from China is as old and traditional as the sweet and sour pork dish given here, which undoubtedly would have been a favorite of both the wealthy man and the peddler.

INGREDIENTS	UTENSILS
6 lean pork chops	paring knife
½ teaspoon salt	medium bowl
3 teaspoons cornstarch	measuring spoons
1 8-ounce can pineapple chunks	saucepan
	large spoon
1 4-ounce jar mixed pickles	large frying pan
2 tablespoons soy sauce	spatula
⅛ teaspoon garlic powder	paper towels
1 medium tomato	serving platter
vegetable oil	small bowl
1 tablespoon water	

1. Turn on oven and set at 200° F.
2. Cut fat off pork chops. Cut meat from bone and into 1-inch cubes. Put meat in a medium bowl and mix with the salt and 1 teaspoon cornstarch. Let stand 20 minutes.
3. Drain pineapple and pour juice into a saucepan. Leave the chunks in the can.
4. Drain pickles and put half of the juice into the saucepan with the pineapple juice. Leave pickles in jar. Stir in soy sauce and garlic powder. Set aside.
5. Cut the tomato into 8 wedges.

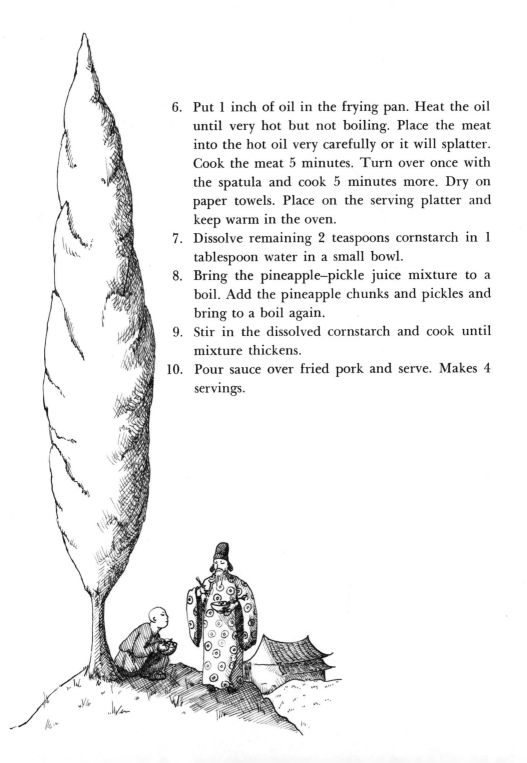

6. Put 1 inch of oil in the frying pan. Heat the oil until very hot but not boiling. Place the meat into the hot oil very carefully or it will splatter. Cook the meat 5 minutes. Turn over once with the spatula and cook 5 minutes more. Dry on paper towels. Place on the serving platter and keep warm in the oven.

7. Dissolve remaining 2 teaspoons cornstarch in 1 tablespoon water in a small bowl.

8. Bring the pineapple–pickle juice mixture to a boil. Add the pineapple chunks and pickles and bring to a boil again.

9. Stir in the dissolved cornstarch and cook until mixture thickens.

10. Pour sauce over fried pork and serve. Makes 4 servings.

The Robbers' Abandoned
Feast of Baked Beans
and Frankfurters

from "The Bremen Town Musicians"

The donkey was too old to haul, the dog and cat were too old to hunt, and the rooster was to be cooked for dinner that night. So they all quickly accepted the donkey's invitation to go to Bremen Town and become musicians in a town band. The donkey would bray, the dog bark, the cat sing, and the rooster crow. But on their way to the town, they came upon a house. The donkey, being the tallest, peeked in.

Inside he saw a table heaped with good things to eat, and a band of robbers enjoying their feast.

Determined to have the dinner for themselves, the animals schemed to drive the bandits away. The dog stood on the donkey's back with the cat on top of him. The rooster perched on the cat. On signal, each let forth with his musical talent. The shattering noise so terrified the thieves that they fled from the house immediately!

The abandoned feast to which the four friends sat down was a wonderful dinner of baked beans and frankfurters, which now you can make—and hopefully eat in peace and quiet.

INGREDIENTS

¼ pound salt pork
2 16-ounce cans of vegetarian
    beans with tomato sauce
1 teaspoon dry mustard
5 tablespoons brown sugar
2 tablespoons molasses
4–6 large frankfurters
2 tablespoons butter or
    margarine

UTENSILS

paring knife
1½-quart casserole dish
medium bowl
large spoon
measuring spoons
large frying pan

1. Turn on oven and set at 350° F.
2. Cut the salt pork into ½-inch cubes. Leave the rind (tough outer skin) on and cut small slashes along it. Put half of the salt pork in the casserole. (Do not substitute bacon, as it changes the flavor of the dish.)
3. In a medium bowl, mix together beans and mustard, brown sugar, and molasses. Pour into the casserole dish.
4. Place the remaining salt pork pieces, rind side up, on the top of the bean mixture.
5. Put casserole in oven and bake for 45 minutes or until it is very hot and the pork pieces are browned.
6. While beans are baking, make four diagonal cuts in the top of each frankfurter.
7. In a large frying pan, melt butter or margarine. Cook frankfurters until nicely browned on all sides. Serve with the hot baked beans. Makes 4 to 6 servings.

The White Bear's Supper of Baked Fillet of Sole in Cream

---

from "East of the Sun and West of the Moon"

A mysterious white polar bear arrived at the door of a poor farmer and requested his youngest and most beautiful daughter in return for a great amount of wealth. Sadly, the girl agreed to go to the bear's exquisite castle in the wild mountains. Once there, he gave her a silver bell to ring for anything that she desired.

She'd had no food since leaving her parents' house and wished for something to eat. So she picked up the silver bell, and scarcely had the first chime sounded when a table appeared, set with the finest meal one could imagine. Never before had the girl tasted such food.

After dinner she went to bed in a beautiful bedroom. There she saw the bear enter the room, lie down on a stone slab, and change into a man. In the morning, he returned to the form of a bear. This happened every night. Soon, the girl became lonely for her family and requested to visit them. The bear told her that she could go but warned her that she must not tell of his two forms. She broke her promise by telling her mother, and so because of this, the bear had to leave to marry an ugly princess in a castle located "east of the Sun and west of the Moon." The girl was determined to find him, and with the help of three hags and the North Wind, she located the castle. There she and the prince out-tricked the court and escaped over the rainbow to happiness.

This delicate fish dish was the first supper the young girl was served after arriving at the white bear's castle.

INGREDIENTS	UTENSILS
1 tablespoon butter or margarine	large shallow baking dish wax paper

5 tablespoons flour

1½ teaspoons salt

¼ teaspoon pepper

4 large sole fillets (boneless
    pieces)

½ teaspoon dry tarragon

3 tablespoons lemon juice

1½ cups heavy cream

measuring spoons

measuring cups

1. Turn on oven and set at 450° F.
2. Butter baking dish with 1 tablespoon butter or margarine.
3. On a large piece of wax paper, mix flour, salt, and pepper.
4. Coat each fillet on both sides with flour mixture, shaking off any excess.
5. Lay fillets in buttered baking dish in one layer, slightly overlapping each other.
6. Sprinkle fillets with tarragon and lemon juice.
7. Pour cream over fillets and bake for 15 minutes. Makes 4 servings.

The Awakening Celebration of Roast Spiced Chicken

from "Sleeping Beauty"

At the banquet celebrating the birth of the princess, all but the most difficult of the thirteen fairies had been invited. Enraged that she had been excluded, the thirteenth fairy went anyway and left a curse that at age fifteen the princess would prick herself and die. Another fairy who had not yet given her gift softened the curse by saying that the princess would not die but sleep for one hundred years. Years later, the curse came true, and the whole castle fell asleep with the princess, including the king and queen, the courtiers, and the animals.

The flies on the wall stopped crawling; the fire on the hearth died down to a whisper, and even the roast meat stopped crackling. The cook, who was pulling the scullion's hair because of some mistake, let him go and went to sleep, and the kitchen maid dropped the hen she had been plucking and laid her head upon her arm.

One hundred years later, a prince passing by noticed the bramble-covered castle and remembered the story of the sleeping beauty from his childhood. Hoping he might find her, he ventured forth to the castle. The heavy weeds parted, the gates opened, and soon he came upon the Sleeping Beauty. His kiss ended the curse, she awoke, and the whole castle came to life. After a few days, a wedding took place. Having waited a century for their happiness, the prince and princess lived a long and happy life.

After the kitchen maid finished plucking the chicken, the cook prepared this delicious dish for the wedding. You will not need to bother with the feathers, but you can certainly pretend that you are a member of royalty.

INGREDIENTS	UTENSILS
3-pound roasting chicken	light string
½ cup beef consommé	roasting pan with rack
1 cup tomato sauce	saucepan
¼ cup cider vinegar or red vinegar	measuring cups
	measuring spoons
1½ tablespoons instant onion flakes	large spoon
	large fork
3 tablespoons Worcestershire sauce	serving platter
	gravy bowl
½ cup honey	
½ teaspoon salt	
1 teaspoon dry mustard	
dash garlic powder	

44

1. Turn on oven and set at 350° F.
2. Wash inside of chicken and pat dry with paper towels. Tie legs together with string.
3. Stir all the other ingredients together in a saucepan. Simmer over low heat for 10 minutes.
4. Spread one-third the sauce over the breast and legs of the chicken. Place in the oven and cook for 30 minutes. Turn over carefully with a large fork so the breast side is down. Spread one-third of the sauce over the back of the chicken and cook for 30 more minutes. Turn over again, spread the remaining sauce over the chicken, and cook for another 30 minutes.
5. Remove chicken to a platter. Pour sauce from bottom of roasting pan into a gravy bowl. Skim off fat with spoon and serve sauce with chicken. Makes 6 servings.

Lamb Chops with Currant Jelly Sauce From the Beast's Kitchen

from "Beauty and the Beast"

Because of an agreement between the Beast and Beauty's father, Beauty lived with the Beast in his grand castle. Although the Beast was truly ugly and she always refused his offer of marriage, she came to welcome his company. Each evening they dined together, and she began to know his virtues of kindness, honesty, and compassion. One evening she asked him how he spent his days.

He raised his rough, fur-covered claws and answered, "I hunt. I prowl the woods for prey. I am an animal, after all, my lady! I must kill for my meat. Unlike you, I cannot eat gracefully."

One day the Beast's magic mirror told Beauty that her father was ill. Her request to visit him was granted, but the Beast warned her that she must return in three weeks or he would

46

die. Beauty returned home and was so happy to be there that she forgot her promise. Then one night she dreamed that the Beast was near death. She fled to him and promised to marry him if he recovered. Suddenly the spell was broken and the Beast became a handsome prince. Naturally, Beauty agreed to marry the prince, and the palace rang with rejoicing.

When the prince was still a beast, his claws could have easily held these delicious lamb chops.

INGREDIENTS	UTENSILS
¼ pound thinly sliced ham	paring knife
¼ cup bread crumbs	wax paper
dash of salt and pepper	measuring cups
4 tablespoons butter or	large frying pan
margarine	measuring spoons
8 thick lamb chops	large spoon
1 cup red currant jelly	platter
2 tablespoons vinegar	saucepan

1. Turn on oven and set at 200° F.
2. Grind or finely chop ham on wax paper. Mix bread crumbs, salt, and pepper together with ham.
3. In a frying pan, melt 2 tablespoons butter or margarine. Brown the lamb chops quickly on each side. You may be able to do four at a time if your pan is big enough.
4. Remove lamb chops and cover each one on both sides with the ham-and-bread-crumb mixture, patting it on with your hands.
5. Add remaining butter or margarine, if necessary, to frying pan. Cook lamb chops about 5 minutes more on each side. Remove to platter and keep warm in oven.
6. In the saucepan, melt currant jelly with vinegar. Pour over chops. Makes 4 servings.

✑ SWEETS AND THINGS ✑

Grandmother's Favorite Chocolate Cupcakes with Rich Chocolate Frosting

from "Little Red Riding Hood"

Little Red Riding Hood was named for the pretty red velvet hood which her grandmother made for her and which she always wore.

One day her mother said to her, "Little Red Riding Hood, here are some cakes and a jar of honey for you to take to Grandmother. She is weak and ill, and they will do her good."

Little Red Riding Hood was told to go directly through the woods to her grandmother's house, but on the way she met up with a wolf. Learning of her errand, the wolf plotted how to eat them both. First he persuaded Little Red Riding Hood to pick some flowers for her grandmother. Then he hurried to her house and ate the kind old woman. When Little Red Riding Hood arrived, she was distressed by the appearance of her grandmother. She asked about her big ears, her big eyes, and finally her big teeth. At the last question, the wolf bounded out of bed and gobbled up Little Red Riding Hood. His hunger satisfied, the wolf fell asleep, but his snoring attracted the attention of the local huntsman. Discovering the crime, he killed the wolf and rescued the grandmother and Little Red Riding Hood.

These chocolate cupcakes are easy to make and are the kind Grandmother really liked best.

INGREDIENTS

1 cup sifted flour
½ teaspoon baking soda
⅛ teaspoon salt

UTENSILS

12-cup muffin tin
measuring cups
sifter

¼ cup powdered unsweet-
ened cocoa

⅓ cup butter or margarine,
softened

¾ cup sugar

1 teaspoon vanilla

2 eggs

½ cup milk

measuring spoons

plate

large bowl

beater

rubber spatula

large spoon

dull knife

cooling rack

1. Turn on oven and set at 350° F.
2. Grease cups of muffin tin with butter and dust each with a bit of flour.
3. Into a sifter, put the sifted flour, baking soda, salt, and cocoa, and sift onto a plate.
4. In a large bowl, beat butter or margarine until light and creamy. Add sugar and vanilla and beat in well.
5. Beat in eggs, one at a time.
6. Beat in half of flour followed by half of milk. Then continue to beat in remaining flour and then milk. Scrape edges of bowl with a rubber spatula so that all the flour is beaten into the batter.
7. Fill each of the cups two-thirds full with the batter.
8. Bake for 25 minutes or until the tops spring back when lightly touched.
9. Run a dull knife around the edges of each cupcake to loosen them. Remove them from muffin tin and cool on a rack. Makes 12 cupcakes.

Chocolate Frosting

INGREDIENTS

3 ounces (3 squares) semi-
   sweet chocolate
¼ cup heavy cream
1 teaspoon sugar
¾ tablespoon butter
shredded coconut or colored
   jimmies (optional)

UTENSILS

saucepan
measuring cups
large spoon, preferably
   wooden
measuring spoons
small bowl

1. Place all ingredients in a saucepan and cook over low heat until chocolate is almost melted. Stir constantly, as chocolate burns very easily.
2. Pour chocolate mixture into a small bowl. Let stand until frosting reaches room temperature.
3. Hold cupcakes upside down and twirl their tops in the frosting. Let drip and then dip them again. Set cupcakes on cooling rack and let frosting set. Decorate with shredded coconut, colored jimmies, or any other topping desired.

The Witch's Gingerbread House Cookies

from "Hansel and Gretel"

The poor woodcutter's second wife disliked her stepchildren, Hansel and Gretel. Since the family was starving, the wife nagged her husband to take the children deep into the forest and let them make their own way. Hansel, learning of this plan, gathered small pebbles and dropped them along the way. After being abandoned, the children followed the pebbles and were soon home. The stepmother was furious and told her husband to take them deeper into the forest. This time Hansel dropped a trail of bread crumbs. The birds ate them, so the children could not find their way home. Suddenly a beautiful white bird appeared and led them to a house made out of wonderful bread with windows of clear sugar.

"Here is where we ought to pitch right in," said Hansel, "and have ourselves a good meal. I'll eat a piece of the roof, Gretel, and you can eat some of the window. The window will taste sweet."

Just as they took their first bites, a witch appeared and lured the children into the house with the intention of eating them. When she was ready to roast Gretel, the little girl outsmarted her and popped *her* into the oven instead. Before they left, the children discovered casks of jewels. Carrying as many as they could, they made their way home. Their father was overjoyed and, as his wife had died, he and the children lived happily ever after.

Delicious gingerbread cookies can easily be made into a small witch's house decorated with frosting and candies. The house is so pretty that you can easily lure your friends to nibble them, just like Hansel and Gretel.

INGREDIENTS

½ cup molasses
¼ cup sugar

UTENSILS

waxed paper
scissors

3 tablespoons butter or
   margarine
1 tablespoon milk
2 cups flour
$\frac{1}{2}$ teaspoon baking soda
$\frac{1}{2}$ teaspoon salt
$\frac{1}{2}$ teaspoon ground nutmeg
$\frac{1}{2}$ teaspoon ground
   cinnamon
$\frac{1}{2}$ teaspoon ground cloves
$\frac{1}{2}$ teaspoon powdered ginger

large cookie sheets
large saucepan
measuring cups
measuring spoons
2 large spoons, 1 wooden,
   preferably
large bowl
bread board
rolling pin
dull knife
metal spatula
cooling racks

1. Trace onto a piece of waxed paper or cardboard the witch's house pattern on the next page. Then cut out the pattern to use as a cookie form.
2. Turn on oven and set at 350° F.
3. Grease cookie sheets.
4. In a large saucepan, bring molasses to a boil. Then add sugar, butter or margarine, and milk. Stir with a wooden spoon until well blended. Turn off heat.
5. In a large bowl, mix flour, baking soda, salt, nutmeg, cinnamon, cloves, and ginger. Stir this mixture into molasses mixture and mix well. Add a few drops of water if necessary to make dough hold together.
6. Sprinkle some flour evenly over the bread board.
7. Place the ball of dough in center of board and roll out into a square about 12 inches on each side and $\frac{1}{4}$ inch thick.
8. Using the cookie form, cut out as many houses as possible,

using a dull knife to cut through the dough. Place the cookie form at several angles to get the most number of houses.

9. With the metal spatula, lift cookies onto greased cookie sheets. Bake in oven for 8 to 10 minutes.

10. Remove onto cooling racks and let cookies harden. Then place on waxed paper to decorate. Makes 4 large cookies (each 6 inches by 5 inches).

Frosting

INGREDIENTS	UTENSILS
⅓ cup butter or margarine, softened	small bowl
⅛ teaspoon salt	measuring cups
2 cups confectioner's sugar	measuring spoons
2 tablespoons cream	beater
food coloring (optional)	custard cups
decorating candies	decorating tube(s)

1. In a small bowl, put butter or margarine and salt. Beat in sugar.
2. Slowly beat in cream.
3. If you want different colors, put some frosting in several custard cups and add a few drops of desired color. Mix coloring in well.
4. Decorate cookies as you wish by putting frosting in decorating tube. If you have only one tube, wash it out carefully each time you change colors. Add candies as you like.

Tom Thumb's
Bread and Butter Pudding
with Candied Fruit

from "Tom Thumb"

A farmer and his wife were very poor, but they would have been happy if they could only have had a child no bigger than the husband's thumb. The farmer heard of Merlin, the famous magician in the Court of King Arthur, and brought this wish to him. By the time the man had returned home, his wife had a tiny son the size of his father's thumb! The Fairy Queen and all the elves attended the christening, and she named the boy Tom Thumb. As Tom grew older, he became mischievous, and his mother had to keep a constant eye on him. One day his mother was making a pudding.

Unfortunately, however, when her back was turned, Tom fell into the bowl, and his mother, not missing him, stirred him up in the pudding, tied it in a cloth, and put it into a pot. The batter filled Tom's mouth and prevented him from calling out, but he no sooner felt the hot water than he kicked and struggled so much that the pudding jumped about in the pot, and his mother, thinking it was be-witched, was nearly frightened out of her wits.

Tom's mother quickly gave the pudding to a passing tinker, who, when it appeared to speak, flung it away. Poor Tom struggled out and ran home to his grieving mother. Tom's adventures of being eaten by a cow, munched on by a giant, and swallowed by a fish finally brought him full circle back to King Arthur's Court, where he became the darling of the royalty.

The English are famous for their puddings, and this recipe is similar to the one Tom fell into. In fact, it is still a favorite of the royal family.

INGREDIENTS	UTENSILS
½ cup chopped candied fruit	2-quart baking dish
½ teaspoon rum flavoring	2 small bowls
½ cup seedless raisins	measuring cups
1 small loaf French bread	measuring spoons
	small strainer

½ stick butter or margarine,   dull knife
    softened   large bowl
2 egg yolks   beater
2 cups milk
2 cups cream
3 whole eggs
½ cup sugar
¼ teaspoon salt
1 teaspoon vanilla

1. Turn on oven and set at 325° F.
2. Butter a baking dish.
3. In one small bowl, mix candied fruit with rum flavoring.
4. In the other bowl, cover raisins with very hot water. Let stand for 5 minutes and then drain off water.
5. Cut ends off French bread and then slice loaf into 10 thin slices. Butter both sides of each slice. Place slices side by side on bottom of baking dish.
6. Sprinkle candied fruit and raisins over bread slices.
7. Separate 2 eggs, putting yolks in a large bowl and saving whites for another recipe.
8. Add yolks, milk, cream, 3 whole eggs, sugar, salt, and vanilla and beat until well mixed.
9. Pour mixture over bread slices. Let stand for 10 minutes to allow bread to soak up custard mixture.
10. Place baking dish in oven and bake for 45 minutes. Serve the pudding warm. Makes 6 servings.

Thumbelina's Honey Ice Cream

from "Thumbelina"

A witch told the old woman who wished for a child to plant the barleycorn she gave her in a flower pot and her wish would come true. Soon the old woman found among the petals of a tulip a beautiful little girl no bigger than her thumb; hence, she named her Thumbelina. However, since Thumbelina was so small, all kinds of trouble lay in store. First, a slimy mother toad kidnapped her for her son, but Thumbelina managed to escape on a floating lily pad pulled by a helpful white butterfly. Then the cockchafer, a grasshopperlike insect, snatched her, but finding her undesirable because she did not look like him, he let her go. Then all through the summer she lived alone in the forest.

She got her food from the honey in the flowers and her drink from the morning dew on the flowers; and in this way, summer and autumn went by.

Thumbelina eventually escaped from her many suitors by flying north nestled in the feathers of the swallow she had at one time nursed back to life. Then she met the tiny and handsome King of the Flowers, who married her and renamed her Maia.

This delicious, delicate ice cream is made from the same honey that Thumbelina found in the flowers.

INGREDIENTS	UTENSILS
1/4 cup water	double boiler
1 teaspoon unflavored gelatin	measuring cups
1 cup milk	measuring spoons
3/4 cup honey	large spoon
1 teaspoon flour	saucepan
1/8 teaspoon salt	2 small bowls
1 egg	fork
2 cups heavy cream	strainer
2 teaspoons vanilla	2 ice-cube trays
	large bowl
	beater
	medium bowl
	rubber spatula

1. Put ¼ cup water in the top of a double boiler. Add gelatin. Stir slightly and let soften for 5 minutes.
2. In a saucepan, heat milk until hot but not boiling.
3. Add milk, honey, flour, and salt to gelatin. Mix well and cook until slightly thickened. Then cover and cook for 10 minutes.
4. Separate the egg, putting the yolk in one small bowl and the white in the other.
5. With a fork, beat egg yolk slightly and slowly add it to honey mixture. Cook for 1 minute longer.
6. Remove cube dividers from 2 ice-cube trays. Strain the mixture into the trays and smooth out the top. Chill in freezer section of refrigerator.
7. Put the chilled mixture from both trays into a large bowl. Beat until very light.
8. With clean, dry beater, beat egg white in small bowl until stiff. Set aside.
9. Pour cream into a medium bowl and whip it with clean beater.
10. Fold egg white into honey mixture. Then fold in whipped cream.
11. Stir in vanilla.
12. Pour the mixture back into ice-cube trays, scraping the bowl clean with spatula. Freeze. Makes 1 quart ice cream.

Marushka's Strawberry Chiffon Pie

from "The Twelve Months"

Because Marushka was a pretty and obedient young girl, her jealous, mean, widowed stepmother and her ugly stepsister, Holena, plotted to kill her. When the January snows were deep, Holena demanded of Marushka some fresh violets. After wandering in the snows for a while, Marushka became lost and followed a light to the mountaintop, where she found the Twelve Months of the Year all dressed in white robes sitting around a fire. Marushka explained her plight, and January, the eldest, asked March to help. The snows melted, spring burst forth, and violets covered the meadows. Marushka picked a nosegay for Holena and returned to give it to her.

The next day, Holena called Marushka again and said, "I long to taste strawberries. Run and fetch me some from the mountain, and see to it that they are sweet and ripe."

Then Marushka sought the help of the months, and June aided her. The snows melted and strawberries grew in the meadows. Holena, now enraged, insisted on fresh apples. September provided autumn and trees laden with apples. Holena, giving up on killing Marushka, set out herself to find the treasured mountain. But she was arrogant to the Twelve Months. The snow fell harder, and the months disappeared, as did Holena and her mother, who ventured out to find her. Rid of the evil stepmother and Holena, Marushka lived happily ever after.

Although you may not have the benefit of June bringing you his strawberries, you can still make this recipe because strawberries are always available.

Pie Shell

INGREDIENTS

1/4 cup butter or margarine
1 1/4 cups graham cracker
   crumbs
1/4 cup sugar

UTENSILS

saucepan
measuring cups
medium bowl
fork
9-inch pie pan
cooling rack

1. Turn on oven and set at 375° F.
2. Melt butter or margarine in a saucepan. Set aside.
3. Mix crumbs and sugar in bowl. Add melted butter or margarine and mix thoroughly with a fork.
4. Put the mixture into the center of the pie pan and with your fingers press firmly to the sides and bottom of the pan. Make a slight rim of crumbs around the top.
5. Bake in the oven for 8 minutes. Cool on rack and then chill in the refrigerator until ready to use. Makes 6 or 7 servings.

Filling

INGREDIENTS

2 cups frozen or fresh straw-
    berries
¾ cup sugar
¾ cup cold water
1 envelope unflavored
    gelatin
1 tablespoon lemon juice
⅛ teaspoon salt
2 egg whites
½ pint heavy cream

UTENSILS

2 medium bowls
measuring cups
paring knife
large spoon
saucepan
measuring spoons
beater
rubber spatula

1. In one medium bowl, slice strawberries and toss with ½ cup sugar.
2. Put the cold water into a saucepan. Sprinkle gelatin over water and let stand for 3 minutes.
3. Add lemon juice, salt, and remaining ¼ cup sugar to gelatin. Cook over medium heat, stirring with spoon until gelatin dissolves. Do not boil.
4. Remove from heat. Cool and stir in sliced strawberries.
5. Chill in refrigerator until mixture forms mounds when dropped from a spoon.
6. Separate eggs, saving yolks for another recipe. Put whites in the other medium bowl.
7. Beat egg whites until stiff. Fold whites into chilled strawberry mixture until no egg white can be seen.
8. Spoon mixture into cooled pie shell. Spread out evenly with spatula. Chill in refrigerator for about 1 hour.
9. When ready to serve, whip heavy cream. Cover top of pie with it.

Cinderella's Wedding Cake with Orange and Lemon Frosting

from "Cinderella"

The glass slipper fit perfectly, so the prince's messenger knew that the beautiful girl, although dressed in rags, was the one with whom the prince had danced and fallen in love at the ball. No one would have guessed she had ever been to a royal ball from the way her cruel stepmother and hateful stepsisters treated her. They demanded she do all the unpleasant household chores. After working, she would always go and sit on the cinders by the fire, earning her the name Cinderella.

One night, Cinderella's Fairy Godmother had waved her magical wand and changed the girl into the beautiful princess who had gone to the royal ball in a gilded carriage made from a pumpkin.

Cinderella went to sit near her stepsisters and paid them a thousand courtesies. She shared with them some oranges and lemons which the young prince had given her.

Now, once the messenger had placed the slipper on Cinderella's foot, her Fairy Godmother arrived and touched her once again

68

with her wand and re-created the beautiful princess of the ball. The prince married Cinderella, and she continued to be good to her stepsisters, helping them to marry into the court.

You can make the happy couple's wedding cake with orange and lemon frosting of the (of that time) rare and precious fruits that the prince gave Cinderella when they first met.

INGREDIENTS	UTENSILS
2 cups plus 2 tablespoons sifted cake flour	3 tiered cake pans (approx. 8″, 7½″, and 6″ in diameter)
1 teaspoon baking powder	measuring cups
½ cup milk	measuring spoons
¼ cup butter	sifter
6 egg yolks	pie pan
1 cup sugar	2 small saucepans
¾ teaspoon vanilla	medium bowl
	beater, preferably electric
	rubber spatula
	3 cooling racks

1. Turn on oven and set at 350° F.
2. Grease well and lightly flour each pan.
3. Sift the cake flour with the baking powder into a pie pan.
4. In one small saucepan, heat milk until very hot, but do not let it boil. Remove from stove and let cool slightly.
5. In the other saucepan, melt butter. Set aside to cool.
6. Separate eggs, putting yolks in a medium bowl. Add sugar

and beat at high speed until mixture is thick and yellow.

7. At a lower speed, beat in milk, vanilla, and then flour mixture.
8. With a rubber spatula, fold in melted butter.
9. Fill each pan ⅓ full.
10. Bake in the oven for approximately 30 minutes or until a toothpick comes out clean after being put into the center of the cake.
11. Cool cakes in pans for 5 minutes before turning them out onto racks. Let them cool completely before frosting. Makes 20 small slices of cake.

Frosting

INGREDIENTS

1 cup butter, at room
    temperature
8 cups confectioner's sugar
¼ cup heavy cream
3 drops orange extract
3 drops lemon extract
1 teaspoon vanilla
1 small package silver petites
bride and groom doll
    decoration (optional)

UTENSILS

medium bowl
beater
measuring cups
measuring spoons
dull knife

1. In a medium bowl, beat butter until light and fluffy.
2. Gradually add sugar to butter and beat until smooth.

3. Stir in cream, orange and lemon extracts, and vanilla into the butter-sugar mixture.
4. Spread frosting with a dull knife on top of the largest cake. Then set the next largest cake on top of the frosting. Frost the top of the second largest cake, and then set the smallest cake on top of that. Frost the top of the smallest cake.
5. Frost the sides of the whole cake, starting from the top so that any excess frosting can be swirled downward. Fill in between the layers with thicker amounts of icing so that no cracks appear.
6. Decorate cake with silver petites. Place bride and groom dolls on top of the cake if you wish.

Pralines from the Fortress of Sweets

from "The Nutcracker"

On Christmas Eve at Maria and Fritz Stahlbaum's home there was a marvelous party of all their parents' friends and their families; but the children's favorite guest was the Stahlbaum children's godfather, Papa Drosselmeyer. His gifts were always mechanical wonders. This year his present to Maria and Fritz was a gallant wooden doll painted as a general.

"Oh, I love him, Godfather," Maria cried. "Did you really make him for us?"

"For you and Fritz, yes. He is a nutcracker. Look! His jaws are so strong that he can crack the hardest nut without hurting his teeth at all."

Arguing over the nutcracker, Fritz broke the doll's jaw, and Maria was put in charge of his care. The party ended, and all were off to bed. But in Maria's room, all were not asleep, and strange events began to happen. Before long the Nutcracker was transformed into a prince. Then he took Maria to meet the Sugar Plum Fairy in the Fortress of Sweets, where a party was given in their honor. The special guests were entertained by lovely music and dancing. Maria awoke on Christmas morning in her own bed, but the Nutcracker, once again a toy, had a peculiar smile on his face. Did all these things really happen— or were they just a dream?

A necessary candy in the Fortress of Sweets would have been pralines, full of rich pecans to remind the prince of his time as a Nutcracker.

INGREDIENTS

4 tablespoons water
2 tablespoons evaporated
   milk
1 tablespoon butter or
   margarine
½ teaspoon salt
4 cups brown sugar
½ teaspoon vanilla
2 cups broken pecans

UTENSILS

3 cookie sheets
waxed paper
saucepan
measuring spoons
measuring cups
wooden spoon
large spoon

1. Line cookie sheets with waxed paper.
2. Put water in a saucepan, and add evaporated milk, butter, salt, brown sugar, and vanilla.
3. Cook over a low heat until butter melts and mixture comes to a boil, stirring constantly with a wooden spoon so that sugar will not burn.
4. When thickened, remove mixture from the heat and stir until slightly cool.
5. Drop 2 tablespoons of candy mixture onto waxed paper, making patties about 3 to 4 inches across. Keep pralines about an inch apart, as they tend to spread.
6. Let candies set and then place in the refrigerator until completely hard. Keep in a tightly covered cookie tin. Makes approximately 18 large pralines.

⊸§ BREADS §⊷

Rumpelstiltskin's Banana Bread

from "Rumpelstiltskin"

A miller once bragged to a greedy king that his beautiful daughter could spin gold out of straw. The king quickly sent for the girl, shut her in a room full of straw with a spinning wheel, and told her that if she valued her life, she must produce the spun gold. As she began to weep, a funny little man appeared and agreed to perform the task if she gave him her necklace. The king later demanded two more miracles, for which the little man's price was the miller's daughter's ring and her first-born child.

The king, delighted with the girl, married her, and she soon gave birth to a heir. The little man came for his reward, but, taking pity on the grieving mother, he gave her three days to guess his name and thus be released from her debt. Messengers were sent throughout the land to gather names, and one reported to the frantic queen that he had witnessed an old little man singing in the woods:

> *"Today do I bake, tomorrow I brew,*
> *The day after that the queen's child comes in,*
> *And oh! I am glad that nobody knew*
> *That the name I am called is Rumpelstiltskin!"*

On the third day, with this information at hand, the queen revealed to the little man his name. Rumpelstiltskin was so furious that he stomped his foot through the floor. That was the last to be seen of him, and the royal child was saved.

Rumpelstiltskin baked once a week. This banana bread could have been the variety he chose on that fateful week, for, once baked, it is a lovely golden color.

INGREDIENTS	UTENSILS
3 medium-sized bananas, overripe	paring knife
	medium bowl
2 cups sifted all-purpose flour	beater
	sifter

1 teaspoon baking soda	measuring cups
1 teaspoon salt	measuring spoons
1 stick butter or margarine,	plate
softened	large bowl
½ cup brown sugar	large spoon
2 eggs	loaf pan
½ cup chopped walnuts	2 cooling racks

1. Turn on oven and set at 350° F.
2. Peel bananas, cut into thirds, and place in a medium bowl. Beat until smooth. Set aside.
3. Place sifted flour in a sifter. Add baking soda and salt and resift onto a plate. Set aside.
4. Place the softened butter or margarine in a large bowl. Beat brown and white sugars into butter, adding each slowly until mixture is light and fluffy.
5. Add eggs to sugar mixture, beating them in one at a time.
6. Add flour mixture and bananas to butter-sugar mixture one-third at a time, beating in well.
7. Stir in chopped walnuts.
8. Pour mixture into greased and floured loaf pan.
9. Bake for 1 hour and 10 minutes or until a toothpick inserted into the middle of the bread comes out clean.
10. Turn baked loaf onto one cooling rack. Place the second rack over bread and quickly turn loaf right side up again. Allow to cool before slicing and serving. This bread can be easily frozen for later use by simply wrapping it tight in foil and keeping it in the freezer. Makes 1 loaf.

The Children's Corn Bread for the Swan

from "The Ugly Duckling"

Suddenly the Ugly Duckling realized that the reflection in the stream was himself. He was not the clumsy, homely duckling that everyone had treated as an outcast because he did not look like any of them. He was a handsome, graceful swan! The bad memories of being rejected by his family, chased by the mean turkey, kicked by the farm maid, and insulted by the old woman's cat and hen were quickly fading. Even the bitter cold winter spent alone in the marsh seemed distant and, in some ways, made him even more appreciative of the happiness and beauty around him.

Some little children came into the garden and threw bread and grain into the water, and the smallest one called out: "There's a new swan!" and the other children joined in with shouts of delight: "Yes, there's a new swan!"

Three of the great swans swam around him several times and then stroked him with their beaks in acceptance. And the old swans bowed before him to acknowledge him as the most regal of them all.

The children could have fed the new swan not only bread crumbs and grain, but as a special treat—corn bread.

INGREDIENTS	UTENSILS
¾ stick butter or margarine	9-inch-square baking pan
1 cup yellow cornmeal	saucepan
½ cup flour	large bowl
1 teaspoon salt	measuring cups
2 tablespoons sugar	measuring spoons
1 cup milk	large spoon
2 eggs	cooling rack
3 teaspoons baking powder	

1. Turn on oven and set at 425° F.
2. Butter the bottom and sides of a square pan.
3. In the saucepan, melt butter carefully over low heat. Set aside.
4. In the large bowl, put cornmeal, flour, salt, sugar, milk,

eggs, baking powder, and melted butter. Beat quickly with spoon until well mixed.

5. Pour mixture into greased pan. Spread out evenly. Bake for 20 minutes. Cool on the rack. Cut into 9 or 12 squares. Serve warm with butter.

✒ GLOSSARY ༄

BAKE: To cook in the oven away from direct flame.

BAKING RACK: A wire rack with small feet that raise it off the counter, used to cool baked goods after they are removed from the oven. The rack allows air to circulate around the cooling food.

BEAT: To work a mixture quickly with a spoon, hand beater, or electric mixer to make it smooth and light. In the case of egg whites, air is beaten into the liquid whites and they become snowy, white mounds that will stand up in stiff peaks when the beater is raised.

BOIL: To cook in a liquid at boiling temperature. During boiling, bubbles constantly rise to the surface of the liquid and break.

CHOP: To cut into small pieces. This is done by cutting the ingredients into manageable pieces first and then cutting these pieces into finer pieces. In the case of an onion, cut off the top and bottom and peel the skin off with a paring knife. Then cut the onion into quarters, and chop the quarters into small pieces.

CORE: To remove the center of the core with the seeds from a whole piece of fruit, usually an apple. Put the apple on a cutting board and insert the corer into the fruit around the core. Turn the corer several times and then pull it out with the core. If the fruit is to be cut, it is easier to cut the fruit in quarters and then cut the core away from each piece of fruit with a paring knife.

CREAM: To beat shortening with a spoon or an electric mixer until it is light and fluffy. Many recipes tell you to work sugar into shortening in this way to get a creamy mixture.

CUBE: To cut into small squares of the same size.

DISSOLVE: To mix a dry ingredient, such as gelatin, into a liquid, such as water, until they are completely combined.

DRAIN: To pour off liquid by putting a food either into a strainer, which has small holes, or into a colander, which is bowl-shaped, stands on feet, and has larger holes. If you want to discard liquid, pour the liquid down the sink, but if you want to save it, pour off the liquid over a bowl.

FOLD: To mix ingredients such as egg whites or whipped cream with a gentle over-and-under motion. The technique is to use a rubber spatula or spoon and cut down through the batter to the bottom of the bowl. Turn the spatula and bring it up against the side of the bowl, folding some of the batter over the egg whites (or whatever ingredient you are folding in). Repeat until the egg whites are thoroughly mixed into the batter.

FRY: To cook in hot fat. To deep-fry is to cook food in a large, deep pan with enough hot fat or salad oil to float the food.

GRATE: To rub food such as a carrot on a grater to make little particles.

GREASE OR BUTTER: To put a small amount of butter, margarine, or oil on a small piece of waxed paper and rub the inside of a baking pan or casserole dish. To *grease and lightly flour* is to first grease or butter the pan and then sprinkle it lightly with flour and turn the utensil so that the flour covers all of the bottom and sides of the pan.

MELT: To heat slowly over low heat in a frying pan or saucepan until it becomes a liquid. Be careful when you melt butter or margarine, as they burn very quickly and then cannot be used.

MIX OR BLEND: To stir ingredients together until they are equally dispersed.

PARE: To cut off the outer skin of a fruit or vegetable, usually with a knife.

PEEL: To pull off the outer skin of a fruit, such as a banana.

ROLL: To spread out dough or pastry with a rolling pin. The technique is to sprinkle some flour on a breadboard to prevent the dough from sticking, and then place the dough on the board. Pat it into a ball and then flatten the ball with your hand. Flour the rolling pin slightly, and begin to roll by pushing the dough out in all directions to form a large circle of thickness and size called for by the recipe.

SEPARATE EGGS: To divide the egg yolk from the egg white. The easiest method is to crack the egg across its middle on the side of a bowl or pan; then catch the yolk in one half of the shell, allowing the white to drop into the bowl. Carefully slip the yolk into the other half of the shell, letting the remaining white drip into the bowl. The sharp edge of the shell helps to cut the white away from the yolk. Be careful not to let *any* yolk get into the white, as the white will not beat up well if you do.

SIFT: To put dry ingredients, such as flour, sugar, and salt, through a flour sifter or fine sieve. In making cakes and pie crust, the flour is sifted twice. You sift the first time (presift) to introduce air, making the flour light. In presifting, always put more than the desired amount of flour into the sifter. If you sift into a pie pan, the flour won't spill over the work area, and you can leave the sifter in the pan without washing it each time you use it. In the second sifting, the measured flour is combined with other dry ingredients.

SIMMER: To cook in a liquid that is just below the boiling point. Tiny bubbles will appear on the surface of the liquid during simmering.

SLICE: To cut into thin, broad pieces.

SOFTEN: To let butter, margarine, or shortening stand at room temperature until soft and easy to use.

TOSS: To gently or lightly mix ingredients such as salad greens with salad dressing or noodles with cheese.

WHIP: To beat rapidly with a rotary beater or electric mixer to trap air in the ingredients. To whip cream, beat very rapidly until it thickens or stiffens. To test, raise the beaters; if the cream mounds and holds its shape, it is whipped. If you're whipping cream in warm weather, be sure to chill your bowl and cream before you start.